# MOUNTAINS

A Buddy Book
by
Fran Howard

**ABDO**
Publishing Company

## VISIT US AT

www.abdopublishing.com

Published by ABDO Publishing Company, 4940 Viking Drive, Edina, Minnesota 55435.

Printed in the United States.

Edited by: Sarah Tieck
Contributing Editor: Michael P. Goecke
Graphic Design: Brady Wise
Image Research: Deb Coldiron, Maria Hosley, Heather Sagisser, Brady Wise
Photographs: Minden Pictures, photos.com

## Library of Congress Cataloging-in-Publication Data

Howard, Fran, 1953-
   Mountains / Fran Howard.
      p. cm. — (Habitats)
  Includes bibliographical references and index.
  ISBN 1-59679-780-0 (10 digit ISBN)
  ISBN 978-1-59679-780-2 (13 digit ISBN)
    1. Mountains—Juvenile literature. I. Title. II. Series: Habitats (Edina, Minn.)

QH87.H69 2006
577.5'3—dc22

                              2005031601

# TABLE OF CONTENTS

What Are Mountains? . . . . . . . . . . . . . .4

Where Are Mountains Found? . . . . . . .6

The Timberline . . . . . . . . . . . . . . . . . .10

Animals Of The Timberline . . . . . . . . .14

Life Below The Timberline . . . . . . . . .20

Why Are Mountain Habitats
Important? . . . . . . . . . . . . . . . . . . . . .26

Fun Facts . . . . . . . . . . . . . . . . . . . . . .30

Important Words . . . . . . . . . . . . . . . .31

Web Sites . . . . . . . . . . . . . . . . . . . . . .31

Index . . . . . . . . . . . . . . . . . . . . . . . . .32

# WHAT ARE MOUNTAINS?

Some mountains are covered with snow.

Mountains are high land **formations**. They are usually larger and higher than hills. Most mountains have steep slopes.

A mountain is one kind of habitat. Habitats are the places where plants and animals find food, water, and places to live. Different plants and animals live in different habitats.

Plants and animals live on mountains all over the world.

Trees and plants grow in the mountains.

# WHERE ARE MOUNTAINS FOUND?

Mountains are found all over the world. They are often found in groups called ranges. The highest part of one mountain is called a peak.

A mountain peak

A mountain range has many peaks.

Green plants growing on the side of a mountain.

Mountains are often found on land. Some mountains are green with flowers, grasses, and trees. Others are covered with snow all year. And, some mountains are too rocky for plants and animals to live.

Mountains are also found in areas covered with water, such as oceans. The world's longest mountain range is in the Atlantic Ocean. This is called the Mid-Atlantic Ridge. The tips of these mountains rise above the water and form islands.

Some islands are mountain peaks.

# THE TIMBERLINE

There are no trees above this mountain's timberline.

Many mountains have a timberline. This is an imaginary line that trees do not grow above. This is because the area above the timberline is too cold for them.

Many plants and trees grow below the timberline.

# Animals Of
# The Timberline

Pikas live in the mountains.

Only certain animals live above the timberline. The air is thinner there because it is so high. Also, it is cold and windy, and there are fewer plants and animals for food.

A mountain goat

Some birds fly high above the mountains, such as golden eagles. These birds eat small animals that live on the mountain.

A golden eagle flying.

A golden eagle

# LIFE BELOW THE TIMBERLINE

Bighorn sheep live in the mountains of North America.

There are a lot of trees, plants, and animals that live below the timberline in the mountains. One reason for this is the warmer temperatures. Also, animals are able to find food and move around more easily.

Some gorillas live in the mountains of Africa.

Giant panda bears live in the mountains of China.

A mountain lion

Panda bears, mountain lions, and brown bears are some of the animals that live below the timberline.

A brown bear

Mountain wildflowers

Trees grow below the timberline. Forests cover mountain slopes. Fields of wildflowers and grasses also grow below the timberline.

A view of the mountains.

# WHY ARE MOUNTAIN HABITATS IMPORTANT?

The animals and plants of mountains need each other. Together they form a **food chain**. Even the smallest plants and animals are part of the food chain.

Mountain Lion                    Elk                    Grass

The Hoover Dam is a famous dam in the United States.

People also need mountains. Mountains get a lot of rain and snow that fills streams and rivers. So, people often build **power** plants in the mountains that are fed by water. This provides electricity for people to use.

Toucans live in the rain forest.

Mountains help maintain weather systems throughout the world. The Amazon Rain Forest exists because of the way air and moisture move toward the mountains.

Mountains are a source of many **minerals**. Gold, silver, and steel are all minerals found in mountainous regions.

People hunt and fish in the mountains. Some people live in the mountains.

Gold is one mineral that is found in mountains.

# MOUNTAINS

- The world's highest mountain is Mount Everest. This mountain is north of India in a mountain range called the Himalayas.

- Many mountains are also volcanoes. Mount Fuji in Japan is a volcano. Mount Rainier in Washington is one, too.

- Bamboo grows in the mountains of China. It is a flowering grass with a hard, hollow stem. Bamboo is one of the fastest growing plants on earth. Bamboo flowers once every 10 to 120 years, depending on the type of bamboo.

# Important Words

**food chain**  the order in which plants and animals feed on each other.

**formation**  something that has been formed into a shape.

**mineral**  a substance found in nature that is not a plant or an animal.

**power**  a form of energy.  Electricity.

# Web Sites

Would you like to learn more about **mountains**? Please visit ABDO Publishing Company on the World Wide Web to find Web site links about **mountains**. These links are routinely monitored and updated to provide the most current information available.

## www.abdopublishing.com

# INDEX

Africa ............................. 21

Amazon Rain Forest ..................... 28

Atlantic Ocean ........................ 9

bamboo ............................. 30

bighorn sheep ........................ 20

brown bear ........................... 23

China ........................... 22, 30

elk ............................... 26

Everest, Mount ........................ 30

Fuji, Mount ........................... 30

golden eagle ...................... 18, 19

gorilla ............................. 21

grasses ...................... 8, 13, 17, 24, 26, 30

Himalayas, the ....................... 30

Hoover Dam .......................... 27

India ............................... 30

Japan .............................. 30

Mid-Atlantic Ridge ...................... 9

minerals ............................ 29

mosses ......................... 13, 17

mountain goat .................... 15, 17

mountain lion .............. 22, 23, 26

panda bear ..................... 22, 23

peak ........................... 6, 7, 9

pika ............................... 14

Rainier, Mount ....................... 30

range .................... 6, 7, 9, 30

shrubs ............................. 13

snow leopard ......................... 17

timberline ............... 10, 11, 12, 13, 14, 17, 20, 23, 24

toucan ............................. 28

trees ............... 5, 8, 10, 11, 20, 24

volcano ............................. 30

Washington .......................... 30

wildflowers ..................... 12, 24

yak ............................ 16, 17

01/08